Tak
Companion Book

by James Ernest and Patrick Rothfuss
Illustrated by Nate Taylor

ISBN 978-1-59100-069-3

Tak Companion Book
by James Ernest and Patrick Rothfuss
Illustrations by Nate Taylor, James Ernest, and Pete Venters

Printed in the USA
First Printing

Contents

Patrick Rothfuss, James Ernest, hot tea, and Tak

Introduction:
Creating an Ancient Game

by Patrick Rothfuss

Y ou hold in your hands a rare and wonderful thing. It's something I had hoped for, but knew would probably never exist. This is the companion book for Tak: a once-fictional game that is now as real as real can be.

I met James Ernest in 2007 at VCON, a fantasy and science fiction convention in Vancouver, BC. We were ships passing in the night. He had no idea who I was, which was fair. I'd been published for less than a year.

But I knew him. I'd been playing James' games for a decade. In fact, I had started playing Cheapass Games at about the same time I started writing *The Name of the Wind*, way back in the beforetimes, the late 1990's.

In 2013, our paths crossed at Origins, a gaming convention in Columbus, and I got to know James a little better. Later that year, he kickstarted a card game called *Get Lucky*, and (at my urging) he was nice enough to give me a cameo in that game.

That collaboration led to our first superhero team up, combining his games and my world in *Pairs*.

Pairs was a "New Classic Pub Game," a simple card game looking for a place to belong. James sent me a test copy, I played it, and I immediately knew that it would be a perfect fit for my world.

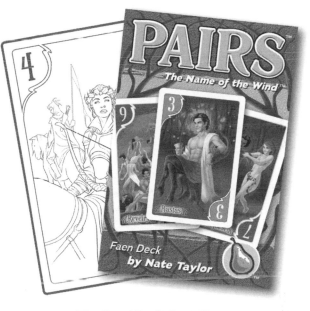

The Faen Deck from Pairs

During the Kickstarter campaign for *Pairs*, James and I offered to create the rules for Tak as a stretch goal. At first I said no, but he kept after me until I agreed to at least discuss the concept with him.

That summer, James reminded me that we had promised to make Tak. He wanted to invent it. He wanted to build the whole thing from the ground up, based on my descriptions in *The Wise Man's Fear*, and all the unwritten stuff in my head.

Again, I said no.

"Why not?" he asked.

"Because," I said. "Tak is supposed to be my world's version of *chess* or *go* or *mancala*. I can't ask you to make a game like that. It's like saying, 'you know those games that have stood the test of time for hundreds of years? The best games ever? Do that thing, but in my world.'

"So first, it's unreasonable for me to ask. Second, you can't do it. No one can. And third, if you did manage to pull if off, nobody would give a crap.

"We're living in the golden age of board games right now. Nobody cares about games like chess any more."

(If you didn't already know this about me, I can be a curmudgeonly bastard.)

"Just let me try," James said. "Let me take a run at it. If you hate what I come up with, we'll never speak of it again."

So I told him, fine. Fine! Do it. Whatever. Jeez.

I feel like I should make it clear that it wasn't that I don't like James Ernest. I do. And it's not that he's not a good game designer. He is. He's brilliant.

The challenge was that up to this point, Tak was a purely mythical game. And while James was great, I figured that nobody could just sit down and make up a game on a par with *chess* or *go*.

My plan was to look politely at whatever game he brought me, smile, and then let him down as gently as possible.

I gave James my Tak notes in November 2014. We met three months later, on the JoCo Cruise, for my first demo game.

I was stunned. This game is everything I wanted. The rules are simple. The strategy is deep. It's more elegant than *chess*. It's more lively than *go*.

I learned to play Tak in about five minutes and I had a blast. More than a year later, I'm still learning. The strategy is unfurling like a flower as I understand more and more about the play of it.

It is, in brief, a beautiful game.

I hope you enjoy it as much as I do.

Patrick Rothfuss
August 2016

▲

Game Rules I:
How to Play Tak

by James Ernest

Tak is a simple two-player strategy game. The goal is to build a *road*, a line of pieces connecting opposite sides of the board.

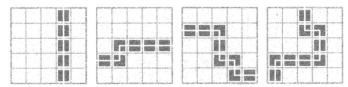

Some examples of winning roads

The Board

You can play Tak on different sizes of board, from 3x3 to 6x6 and higher. The board on the back of this book is a "hybrid 5x5" board, meaning that it can be used for any size game up to 5x5.

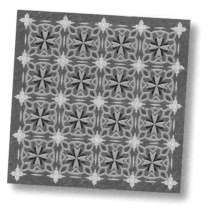

To play a 5x5 game, use the 25 diamonds. For a 4x4 game, play on the 16 squares. For a 3x3 game, use just the inner nine diamonds.

Tak boards can be 3x3, 4x4, 6x6, 8x8, or even larger. The "Classic Set," the first retail edition of Tak, includes a double-sided 6x6 board.

Connections: Spaces on the board are connected only by their edges. In Tak, things are not adjacent diagonally, and pieces do not move diagonally.

Cardinal Directions: In examples, it is sometimes helpful to use cardinal directions (north, south, east, west) to describe movement or placement. These directions are not actually on the board.

The Pieces

In a 5x5 game, each player uses 21 standard pieces called "stones," plus one special piece called the "capstone." Stones can be played in two ways: *flat* and *standing*.

Flat Stones: Most stones will be played flat. In this orientation, they are called "flat stones" or just "flats." Flat stones can stack up, as a result of movement (see below).

Standing Stones: If a stone is played on end, like this, it is a "standing stone" or "wall." Nothing can be stacked on a standing stone, and it does not count as part of a road.

Capstones: Capstones embody the better aspects of both standing and flat stones: they *do* count as part of a road, but they *can't* have another piece stacked on top. In addition, a capstone by itself has the ability to *flatten a standing stone.*

Setting Up

The board starts empty. All pieces begin in the player's "reserve," which just means the pieces that are not yet on the board.

The number of pieces each player uses is based on the size of the board:

Board Size:	3x3	4x4	5x5	6x6	8x8
Stones:	10	15	21	30	50
Capstones:	0	0	1	1	2

Note that capstones are used only on boards of size 5x5 and higher. Also, there are no numbers for 7x7, because it is rarely played.

Starting Player: In your first game, determine randomly who will go first. In subsequent games, take turns going first.

The First Turn: On the first turn, each player will place one of their *opponent's* stones. You may play this stone in any empty space, and it must be played flat. After the first turn, play proceeds normally. *Example: if White goes first, White plays a Black stone, then Black plays a White stone, then White takes the first normal turn.*

The Goal

The object is to create a line of your pieces, called a *road*, connecting two opposite sides of the board. The road does not have to be a straight line. Below is an example of a winning road.

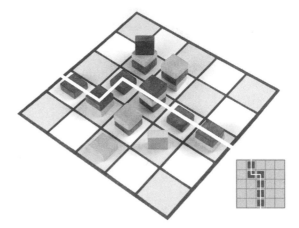

A winning road for Black

In the example above, Black has won the game by connecting two opposite sides of the board with a road. Each space along this path has a stack with a black flat stone on top.

Other Victory Conditions

Flat Win: If either player runs out of pieces, or if the board is completely covered, then the game ends immediately and the player with the most flat stones (on top of stacks) wins. If this count is tied, then the game is a draw.

Double Road: If a player creates a winning road for both players with the same move, then *the active player* is the winner. (This is quite rare.)

On Each Turn

On your turn you may either *place* a piece in an empty space, or *move* one of the stacks under your control.

If you place your last piece, or if you fill the last space on the board, the game ends immediately. See *Winning the Game*, below.

Place: You can place a flat stone, a standing stone, or your capstone in any *empty space* on the board. *(You never play a piece directly on another one. Stacks form only as a result of movement.)*

Move: You can move one or more pieces in a stack that you control. A "stack" of pieces can be any height, including just one piece. "Control" means that your piece is on top.

To move the stack, take any number of pieces off the top (up to the *carry limit*, defined below), and move them in a straight line (but not diagonally), dropping *at least one piece* off the bottom in each space along the way.

The pieces that you drop will cover up any stacks that are already there.

Standing stones and capstones cannot be covered, which means that all the spaces in your path must either be empty or contain flat stones.

A capstone can, by itself, move onto a standing stone and flatten it. An example of this type of move is given below.

Movement Examples

Understanding movement is the key to the game, so below are three examples of how pieces move.

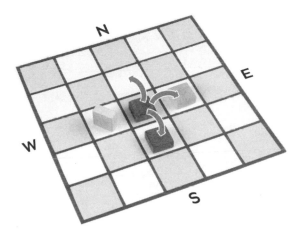

Moving One Piece: The black piece in the example above can move to three of the four adjacent spaces as indicated.

If it moves *north*, it moves into an empty space. If it moves *east*, it covers a white piece. If it moves *south*, it covers a black piece. It cannot move *west*, because that space is occupied by a standing stone.

Standing stones and capstones move in the same way as flat stones. If this piece were a capstone, it would also have the option to move *west*, flattening the standing stone there and covering it.

Because you must drop at least one piece in each space as you go, a stack of a single piece can move only one space. Taller stacks can move farther, as shown in the next examples.

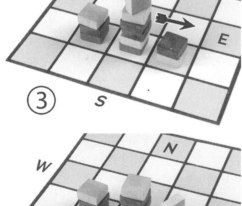

Moving a Taller Stack: At left is an example of making a move with a taller stack. White controls this stack, with a standing stone on top. She decides to move east. (Movement is always in a straight line.)

1: White can take as many as five pieces off the top of this stack. (*See carry limit, below.*) That's the whole stack, and she decides to take it all. She could also have left one or more pieces behind.

In each space along the path, White must drop *at least one piece*. These pieces come off the bottom of the stack.

2: In the first space, she decides to drop two pieces, which will leave her in control of that space. She carries the remaining three pieces onward.

3: On the second space, White decides to drop two pieces again. This will give her control of this stack as well.

4: She moves only the top piece, the standing stone, into the last space. The end result of this move is shown in figure 4.

This single move gave White control of all three spaces, leaving Black in control of no spaces at all!

The rest of this board is empty, to make the example more clear. In a normal game, Black would probably still have control of some other spaces.

But it's not impossible for a move like this to happen in a real game. If that were the case, Black could not *move* on the next turn, since he controls no stacks; he would have to *place* a new piece.

Tall stacks are quite versatile. White had *many* other options with this stack. She could have moved it to the north or south, or she could have left different numbers of pieces in each position.

Moving Capstones: Capstones move like any other piece, except that they have one extra option: By itself, a capstone can *flatten* a standing stone. In this example, Black will move his capstone two steps, to flatten White's standing stone.

1: Black could move up to five of the pieces in this stack, but he elects to leave two pieces behind, and move just three pieces (the capstone and the two beneath it) to the next space. This leaves a black stone in control of the original space.

2: To flatten the standing stone, the capstone will have to act alone. So Black leaves the other pieces on the middle space, and moves the capstone by itself onto the standing stone.

3: Figure 3 shows the end result of this move. Black has flattened White's standing stone, but has left White in control of the middle stack. This is not perfect for Black, but this is fairly common, because capstones often end up on top of pieces of the opposite color. The end position shows why: Black has flattened White's standing stone, so he again finds his capstone atop a White flat.

Note that capstones can flatten stones of *either color* (not just the opponent's color).

As in the previous example, the player had many options for what pieces to leave where. The only requirement was that in order to flatten the standing stone, the capstone had to finish alone.

Calling "Tak": There are two schools of thought on calling "Tak." This is simply a warning to your opponent that you are one move away from winning. Some players believe it is unnecessary, and even counterproductive. Others believe it is an essential courtesy, and that not calling "Tak" goes against the fundamental spirit of the game.

Neither of these opinions is completely without merit, and the decision falls to the style of each player group as to what is best for your game. For more, see "Courtly vs. Street Tak" on page 29.

Additional Movement Rules

Carry Limit and Stack Height: There is no upper limit to the height of a stack. However, there is a limit to the number of pieces you can move *off* of a stack, called the "carry limit."

The carry limit is always equal to the width of the board. So, in a 5x5 game, the largest number of pieces that you can carry is five. That means if you start with a stack of 7, you must leave at least 2 of those pieces in the starting position.

Insurmountable Pieces: Neither a capstone nor a standing stone can have a piece stacked on top of it (except that a capstone can flatten a standing stone). These pieces place and move normally, but can't be stacked upon. Therefore, it's illegal to make a move that would place a piece atop these types of pieces.

Flattening Stones: The capstone can move onto a standing stone, flattening it. A standing stone can be flattened only by the capstone by itself, not by a taller stack with the capstone on top.

A capstone can make a longer move (with a taller stack) before flattening a standing stone, as in the example on page 7, but the capstone must be the only piece that moves onto the standing stone.

A capstone can flatten a standing stone of either color.

Aside from flattening it with a capstone, you cannot lay down a standing stone.

Winning the Game

The goal of the game is to create a *road*, which is a line of pieces that joins opposite edges of the board (north to south or east to west). This is called a "road win."

A road is mainly composed of flat stones. Your capstone can also be part of a road, but standing stones cannot. If either player has a road, the game is over and that player wins.

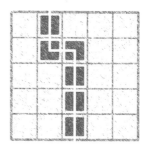

Flat Win: The game also ends if the board is *full*, or if either player runs out of pieces. "Full" means that there are no empty spaces on the board.

As soon as either player fills the last board space, or plays their last piece, the game is over. If no one has a road at this point, then the winner is determined by counting the flat stones. This is called a "flat win."

Count only the flat stones *on top* of all the stacks on the board. Standing stones and capstones are not counted, nor are flat stones that are covered.

If this count is tied, then the game is a draw.

Double Road: If a single move completes a road for both players, then the active player wins. *For example, if White makes a move that creates a white road and a black road, then White wins because it is White's turn.*

Scoring

Scoring is not strictly necessary, but it is a good way to track your results over several games.

Because there is a slight advantage for the player who goes first, it's most equitable to play an even number of games, alternating who goes first.

Your score for winning is equal to the size of the board (for example, 25 points in a 5x5 game), plus the number of pieces that remain in your reserve.

For example, in a 4x4 game, if you win the game with 4 unplayed pieces, you score 20 points. This is 16 points for the board, and 4 for the pieces.

Using this system, you will score more points by winning more efficiently.

Basic Strategy

You can learn the basics on a smaller board. 3x3 is actually a little weird, so most people learn on 4x4.

When you play 4x4, you have only 15 stones per side, and no capstone. This quick-playing game lets you learn the *offensive* abilities of standing stones.

Most of the stones you play will be flat.

In most games, you should expect the first few rounds to involve placing, not moving, because it's advantageous to get more pieces into play. However, there will come a time when you need to make a move, or place a wall, because a flat stone won't accomplish what you want.

Players are often just one or two moves away from winning. Some threats are easy to neutralize, and others are harder (or impossible). Obviously your strategy should be to answer your opponent's threats while developing your own.

Strength builds in stacks. You must play new pieces in empty spaces, so stacks will only form as a result of movement. When you create a stack, pay attention to where it can move, and what other pieces it can cover and control.

When you advance to the 5x5 or 6x6 game, you'll introduce the capstone. Capstones are powerful when they get some range, so try to get them onto a tall stack, ideally comprised mostly of your own pieces. A capstone can't be fully neutralized, but it can be isolated and blocked.

Playing Without a Board

Tak is a super-portable game, especially if you learn to play without a board.

Fancy Tak sets include boards of one kind or another: sturdy wooden boards, versatile leather boards, or boards painted onto cloth squares.

Any decent tavern should have a 5x5 Tak board, or, in the less refined establishments, a board may be scratched into a tabletop. Failing that, one can always mark out a grid with a few lines of chalk.

But it's even more common for people who find themselves without a board simply to mark the center of the board, and imagine the rest.

For a 4x4 or 5x5 game, this is pretty easy. Choose a knot in the tabletop, a scrap of paper, or a nice flat coin to designate the center space. As the pieces accumulate around the center space, the entire board becomes clearly delineated.

If you're lucky enough to own a Tak coin, like the ones shown above, you can use it to designate the center space of a 5x5 grid (left), or to mark the center intersection of a 4x4 grid (right).

The Road to Tinuë:
A History of Tak

by Daramin Centes

Welcome.

What you hold in your hands is the pure child of my mind. For more than a year's time I have labored to produce a monograph on Tak like none other in existence.

Never before has a single work attempted to bring together so many diverse sources in an attempt to illuminate the history, strategy, and culture surrounding Tak.

It is my hope that it may provide a useful resource to future scholars, current enthusiasts, as well as new players curious about this, the noblest of games.

Quiant Eteariam Ve!

Re'lar Daramin Centes Esq.
Fourth Tier Scriv. Order of the Yew

Tak is an ancient game, older than empires. For centuries, its simple rules and deep strategies have captured the hearts and minds of players throughout the Four Corners and doubtless into the barbarous lands beyond. It is not for nothing that famed strategist Peyramo Dolsn referred to Tak as "King of games, and the game of Kings."

It has always struck me as unfortunate that so much of the best writing on Tak is scattered. Many of our greatest thinkers have opined on the game, and there are mentions spread through dozens on dozens of volumes on tactics, history, arithmetic, and etiquette. But many of those books are woefully inaccessible to the common man. They are badly translated, overwritten, or simply impossible to discover without access to private collections or many hours in the deep stacks.

There has been much written of Tak lately, spurred by the work of Maris Cintor and those that have followed in her footsteps. It is thanks to her scholarship that we have an increasingly accurate understanding of the origins of Tak, and can look back with better clarity than ever before through two millennia to where it all began.

In this monograph, I have worked to bring together all that is best from those essential sources. I am fortunate to have a gift for languages, so I have been able to include works inaccessible to those without the stomach or intellectual fortitude required for translation and therefore true scholarship.

Having gleaned the best from history, I will strive to combine this information with newer writings, theories, strategies, and research that has only recently come to light.

It is my hope that, for beginners, this book will serve as a primer and introduction to Tak. For experienced players, I hope this will be a unique resource that contains all that is essential and perhaps offers some unique insight into the play, strategy, and history of this game.

As Feltemi himself mentions, we always have one foot in the past. So let us begin at the beginning: 2000 years ago in the lands that would eventually be known as Modeg and Ademre.

We will start by examining games like *Kaen* and *Locke* that evolved into *Trio* and *Taket* before finally culminating in the perfect pearl of a game that we know and love.

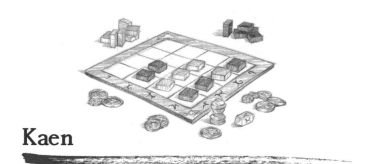

Kaen

Kaen, also known as "From the Earth to the Sky," is a dice-based board game at least 2000 years old, with historical references dating back as far as the earliest recorded days of the Modegan royal line.

Kaen was played by soldiers and guardsmen in the early chaotic days that surrounded the formation of the *Carashen Dominate*. It is likely due to wartime mingling with mercenary troops that the game spread beyond the borders of what is now Modeg. If, in fact, it originated there at all.

The earliest surviving mention of Kaen is in the disciplinary record of a strahl, who was forced to punish her troops for neglecting their duties. She refers to the game harshly, and explains:

> *"I would rather my troops suffer from the flux than be afflicted with* Kaen. *This is because a soldier will eventually purge himself clean given a dozen days, or, barring that, have the decency to die. But once [a thain] has pricked his fingers on this game, it will plague him forever."*

From this description, we can assume that *Kaen* was quite popular. What's more, it seems it was not viewed kindly by the upper reaches of society.

Or, at the very least, that this commander was not particularly skilled at the game.

In Kaen, the object is to create a *bridge* that connects opposite sides of the board, similar to the road win in Tak. However, pieces in Kaen do not move or stack, and the player does not have a free choice of where to place his stones. Instead, the roll of a 4-sided die (called a *Hut*) dictates where stones can be placed.

Historians agree that the earliest Huts were little more than modified caltrops, like the ones shown at right.

Ancient examples have been found in armories, soldiers' graves, and the foundations of ruined towns, and predate any written record of the game by several hundred years.

A more stylized Hut is shown at left: it is a simple four-sided barrel die, marked with the numbers 1 through 4. These marks can be simple dots, but more often they are glyphs representing those numbers. A common glyph set is shown below.

<table>
<tr><td>𐍈</td><td>𐌾</td><td>𐌲</td><td>ʼ</td></tr>
<tr><td>Arex</td><td>Dog</td><td>Cat</td><td>Staff</td></tr>
</table>

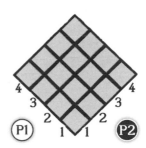

The Kaen board is a diamond shape, as shown here, with each player's symbols running from the center bottom and up their edge. These symbols correspond to the markings on the hut.

Kaen was typically played using common objects such as stones, coins, or shells, though it can also be played with Tak pieces. It was usually played on makeshift boards, or with no board at all. Very few complete Kaen sets survive today, but the game is occasionally mentioned in the literature of the time, most notably in the *Varnisads*.

Though some players used decorative doubling markers, these were often common objects such as buttons or beads. The Hut was the only special piece required for the game. Huts were sometimes carved from wood or bone, and some examples of this piece still survive today. There are a few surprisingly elegant examples, indicating that Kaen was not exclusive to the lower classes.

Versions of Kaen are still played in Modeg and throughout the small kingdoms today.

The game is also known by the names of *Kaene* and *High Bridge*. It is believed to have given rise to a family of dice-based gambling games too numerous for this volume.

Note: The full rules for Kaen, describing the most widely accepted modern version of the ancient rules, are given later in this book.

Locke

Locke is a quick-playing board game that uses a 5x5 board with ten pieces per player. *Locke* has its roots among the Ademre, and is still played there, though not widely.

Without any piece as distinctive as a Hut, there is little artifact evidence of Locke, which gives us few hints to the true age of the game.

Similarly, the nomadic nature of the Ademre before their settlement in northern Stormwal means that written records from that time period are not just rare, they are nonexistent.

The earliest known mention of a game similar to Locke is in Delitari's *Cemopendia*, so we can show the game to be at least 1200 years old. But most scholars believe it to be much older than that.

From what we can find, the ancient game of *Locke* seems quite similar to the game that is played in Ademre today. But with virtually no textual referents, this assumption is entirely speculative.

Locke is a strategy game in which pieces can move and combine into stacks. The goal is to occupy any three spaces along the center line.

Note: The full rules to Locke are given later in this book.

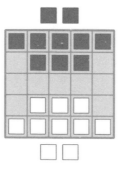

Trio

The oldest known game that closely resembles modern Tak comes from Venumet, roughly 700 years ago. Predating any other known mentions by more than a hundred years, the game of *Trio* was first described in the journal of the infamous Yllish explorer Farau Lyari.

Although we have several complete Trio sets from various locations and time periods, the game is no longer played, and the rules are a subject of conjecture. If it were not for Farau's description of the games he played against Avara, the daughter of his host, we would have very little information on this game at all.

In his journal, Farau describes a game similar to Locke, using a 5x5 board and turn-based placement of stones. The game uses stacks of pieces, like Locke, but it's clear that players were allowed to stack their own pieces on top of their *opponent's* pieces, creating a new kind of game play.

Farau's journal is useful, but it is important to note that he dwells more on Avara's charms and their flirtatious conversation rather than on the rules of the game. This is hardly surprising.

While Farau's journals are a boon to historians and scholars, Farau himself was neither. Let us be honest and know the man for what he was, a scoundrel and a braggart with the morals of a feral cat, albeit one with a clever quill.

Yllish frailties aside, we owe quite a bit to his bawdy nature in this particular instance, as it brings us unique information as to the nature of the game:

Wresting my eyes from her, I considered the board briefly, then moved again, positioning the large, round stone atop my stack of pieces.

"You're beginning to see," Avara said, nodding her approval. "It is not enough to have it in play. The more stones it tops, the more powerful it is."

I smiled at her. "So again the game reflects the world."

She met my eyes in a direct manner that I found at once startling and appealing, then moved again, sliding a stack of her own stones across the board. "Yes," she said. "But the proof is in the use of a thing…"

"It is a shame that after I make use of it, it falls." I spread my stones in a line, ending with the round stone on top of her own stack. "But fear not, I shall make it rise up again."

Throughout this innuendo-laden conversation, several features of the game become apparent.

Farau mentions "a large, round stone" that could be played on top of a stack, which may have made it illegal to add more small stones. This suggests a new kind of piece which acts somewhat like a modern Capstone or standing stone.

Farau also describes an action he calls both a "fall" and elsewhere a "tumble," suggesting a Tak-style run-out of a stack of pieces.

The journal also mentions "earth and sky" several times when describing the end of a game, which is a strong indication that a Kaen-style road-based win had replaced the simple "occupy the center line" goal of Locke.

With these clues, we see a game in which the movement-based strategy of Locke is combined with the road-based victory condition of Kaen, but without further study we cannot reconstitute a full set of rules for Trio.

The Road to Tinuë: A History of Tak

Taket

For the devoted historian and scholar, the most maddening of all Tak antecedents is the game commonly known as Taket. It is barely half the age of Kaen and Locke, but we know far less about it.

Mentions of Taket appear in literature, folk songs, court records, and other documents spanning centuries. But despite all of this, the details of the rules are rarely mentioned, and so the particulars of the game remain a mystery to this day.

Taket is the first game in which we see an explicit mention of variable board size. Taket boards survive in 4x4, 5x5, and 6x6 sizes, with sets of stones ranging between 10 and 30 pieces to a side. In this way and several others, the game seems closely related to modern Tak, but probably without capstones, and with several other notable differences.

Most of our knowledge of the game rules can be found in court records from Tinuë, detailing a vicious Taket game between a brewer and tanner. They were each the head of their own guild, which probably explains why the trial was so extensive and the records so detailed.

The two litigants spent the better part of a week engaged in a cutthroat series of Taket games. Stakes were high, and at the end involved the deed to an entire meadery.

When the brewer lost the deed, he turned to the courts to dispute the legitimacy of the game and regain his property.

From these notes, and other documents from the same era, we get a muddy but interesting picture of the rules for Taket.

In Taket, players seem to have started with some pieces on the board, as in Locke, though their exact configuration is not known. This may have varied by region, and may also have been different for the first and second player.

Some modern scholars theorize that the location and number of pieces on the board may have incorporated a handicapping system, but there is not enough information to substantiate this.

Partial Taket sets survive in various materials and sizes. Hard leather boards, reversible with a 6x6 pattern on the obverse and 5x5 on the reverse, are fairly common. Surviving sets include pieces of carved stone, wood, and precious metals.

Others claim that this passage does not disagree with the modern rule, and that all stones were the same type of piece, and played by the same rules, but that because of their irregular shapes, some of them simply could not support other pieces.

It is well documented that players carried their own personal sets of stones for Taket, perhaps (as suggested above) with a customized mix of standing and flat stones.

Traditionally, each player brought only his own pieces to the game, not enough for both players. The assumption was that anyone who knew the game would also carry his or her own half-set.

There is some mention of "taking the blind," or playing with your opponent's pieces, which means that while a player might configure her own set to her personal style of play, her opponent always had the option to "take the blind" and swap piece sets.

To a modern sensibility this seems somewhat absurd since if one "takes the blind," he also forces his opponent to play with his own set, which could be engineered to play terribly. So there are obviously aspects of this custom that we don't fully understand.

Today, the practice of carrying one's own half-set has mostly disappeared, and Tak sets include a full two-player complement of pieces. But the modern tradition of carrying a unique and individual capstone seems to stem from the personal sets of stones in Taket.

But the strange variety of piece sets is baffling, seeming to have neither a consistent number of pieces nor shapes. Given this, it is impossible to know how many pieces were used, or even if there was a common standard.

Another tantalizing clue to the details of Taket is found in Merina's biography of Maern Louce. He mentions an occasion in which, in a game of "Takt" between the court composer and his mistress, she "runs short of standing pieces."

Some Tak scholars interpret this offhand phrase as clear evidence of two distinctly different kinds of piece, including normal and "standing" stones.

Modegan Tak

The first game that we can call nearly identical to modern Tak is the Modegan game also called Tak, which was probably a descendant of Taket.

Modegan Tak was described by Enile Lanuet, in her seminal but awkwardly titled *Games and Wars*.

In this volume she includes not only full rules for the game, but a lengthy strategy document and several clear illustrations of historical and otherwise notable games.

Lanuet claims in no uncertain terms that the game is of Modegan origin, and hers is the eldest detailed written reference by a span of 80 years.

It may be wrong to read any particular historical significance into this fact, as other such records doubtless existed, but were lost in the burning of Caluptena.

While we know the game itself is Modegan, our historical knowledge of it is colored by the fact that it rose to prominence in the Court of Verian Loeclos at a time many consider the high point of the power of Tinuë and its attendant court and kingdom.

Whatever the game's origin, the fact that Tak was popular in this particular time and place is hugely significant.

Not only was Tinuë a shining beacon for art and education during the reign of Verian, but the city was also an unparalleled hub of economic, political, and military power.

Much as roving mercenaries carried Kaen with them and spread it like the flux, so did merchants, courtiers, and scholars carry Modegan Tak from Tinuë out into the world.

In addition to describing the rules of play, Lanuet also gives names to many of the strategies and gambits. It says a great deal that, even now, it is through her treatise that many modern players learn their strategy, as well as game terms such as Hunters, Tumblers, Reserves, and so forth.

Of course, since then, some rules have changed. And one must admit that even the modern game of Tak can be said to be multiple games, both in etiquette and in the written rules.

The rules to Modegan Tak can best be summed up by its few differences with the modern game. To wit:

Board and Pieces: The only board sizes are 4x4, 5x5 and 6x6. All games include one capstone.

First Turn: White always goes first. Players play their own piece on the first turn.

Starting Player: The loser of the game takes the white pieces (and the lead) in the next game.

Draws: If the game is a draw, Black wins.

Terms and Phrases:
The Language of Tak

Players new to Tak can often be confronted with a great deal of new terminology, above and beyond that which is required to actually play the game. Below is a list of common game terms and Tak-related colloquialisms that may help ease your way into the community of players.

For the scholarly among you, I have included some notes on the regionality of the terms, and extended some of my own theories as to their etymological origins.

Aturan Start: To start the game by throwing each player's first piece onto the board, intended to give the game a more random start. Traditionally one throws one's own piece, not the opponent's.

Brooker's Fall: To run out a tall stack in order to crush one of your own standing stones with your capstone, creating a more powerful and strategically advantageous piece.

Caning: In phrases like "Getting Caned" or "Taking a Caning" this refers to being badly beaten. Specifically, a humiliating defeat delivered by an opponent with less experience, or someone of lower intellect or social class.

Doubtless this is an old piece of slang referring to being beaten by a rustic opponent who could only afford a homemade set of cane pieces.

Captives: Pieces of the opposite color that are contained within a stack. Also called *Prisoners*. (Pieces of the same color are called *Reserves, q.v.*)

The stack pictured at right is controlled by Black, and contains two white *captives* and one black *reserve*.

Coverage: Roughly, the proportion of enemy pieces that are captive. "High coverage" means that a large ratio of enemy pieces are in stacks under your control.

Crushing: The act of a capstone moving onto a standing stone and converting it into a flat stone. Also *Toppling* or *Flattening*.

Guard: A standing stone placed near a stack as a blocker, usually to keep a capstone from moving to its full reach.

Hawking: Capturing a stack of your opponent's stones (over several turns) by gathering them up with a standing stone or capstone. This is a gambit overtly intended to collect a large number of captives. This term appears to be regional to the Commonwealth.

Hipper: *(archaic)* A very tall stack of pieces that greatly exceeds the carry limit of the board. Also occasionally called a *Tall Tower*.

Hunter: A stack of two same-color stones. Also called a *Thane* (Vintas) or a *Strahl* (Modeg).

Fall: Another word for moving a tall stack (see *Brooker's Fall*). Sometimes also called a *Slide*.

Foot: A connection to the edge of the board. Based on "foothold." To "lose a foot" is to lose or sacrifice one's connection to an edge.

Lady: A stack of pieces, usually at least three high, topped by a capstone and a piece of matching color. This is a powerful stack which takes some effort to construct. Also referred to as a *Proud Lady*, a *Pike*, a *Stripe* (Vintas), or a *Cimbrel* (Modeg).

Leg Over: A quick, early-game win, in which a player essentially covers all or nearly all enemy pieces, surprising an inexperienced player.

Lug: A strategically impotent capstone, so called due to its location in a distant part of the board, inability to move, etc. "Lugging" means trying to get this piece into a better position.

Marred Tower: A tall stack topped by a wall, especially one where the wall is directly atop the opposite color. Also *Married*. *One might suspect that the term "Married" references the alternating colors of the pieces. Or that it is "Marred" by being less powerful than the Lady. However, it is my suspicion that this is actually a corruption of the Modegan word "Amari."*

Merk: To defeat an opponent without using your capstone. This concept seems to be one of the most common in the game, with many regional variants. Also *Routed*, *Shut Out*, *Haket* (Siaru), or *Asaou* (Modegan).

Ever the sensationalist, Geoffrey Monmut implies that "Getting Merked" is a derogatory term that derives from the word "Merkin." Unfortunately, his theory tells us more about Monmut's personal history and proclivities than it does the history of the word itself.

A much more reasonable (though still unlikely) explanation comes from one of Maris Cintor's first works on Tak, where she suggests the term derives from the Ademic "Amarke," a dueling term that refers to striking your enemy so quickly that the blow lands before they can ready their own weapon.

It is with deference and respect that I offer my own suggestion, that this term refers to the infamous Breon Mercer, who traveled the world living by his wits and his winnings from Tak. Reportedly, Mercer was capable of playing the subtlest of courtly games, but when money was on the line, he was known to eschew the niceties of play, and destroy his opponents with astonishing tactical brutality.

Palace: A 2x2 arrangement of flat stones of the same color. Commonly believed to be a strong, versatile configuration. Also called a *Castle* or *Fort*. *Given the ubiquity of military terms, I suspect the term "palace" to be a corruption of "palisade" rather than a reference to a royal estate.*

Pocket: A strategically powerful empty space, next to two tall stacks. Coined to describe a good location to place a wall or capstone. Also called a *Tuck* (archaic.)

Reach: Of a stack of pieces, the distance that the top stone can move. Taller stacks have more reach.

Reserves: Pieces contained within a stack that is controlled by the same color. (See *Captives*.)

Running Out: Moving a tall stack a long distance, usually to complete a road.

Skinning: To delay a loss through the excessive or desperate play of standing stones. This strategy can prevent any roads from being complete, and thus force the opponent into a lesser-valued flat win. Also "Skin the Game."

In his recent work on Tak, Geoffrey Monmut proposes that this term originates from someone avoiding a loss by the "skin of his teeth." While Monmut's attempt to engage in serious etymology is laudable, he should leave it to those with proper training. This term obviously derives from the "Temskin Wall."

As a linguist, I feel obliged to point out that Baronet Temskin was Veltish, and therefore the "S" in his name was silent. However, most people reading Enile Lanuet's work in various flawed translations would have no way of knowing this, so Monmut's mistake is understandable, if not acceptable.

Stone: In some regions, "Stone" refers only to the flat or standing piece, while "Piece" includes stones and capstones. Elsewhere, "Stone" is the preferred term for all types of Tak piece.

Taking the Blind: This is an older custom of choosing to play with your opponent's pieces, from a time when each player carried their own set.

Temskin Wall: A line of standing stones that completely prevents an opponent from making a road. *One of Lanuet's original terms, this is named for a Baronet who used this strategy frequently and to good effect. While technically this applies only to a board that is completely walled off, it is frequently used to describe a less-effective strategy from any wall-heavy opponent.*

Trifoil: A double road win that simultaneously connects all four edges of the board. Not technically better than a normal road win, but infinitely more showy.

Tumbler: A tall stack with a capstone atop a piece of the opposite color. This type of stack is more common but less powerful than a *Lady*.

Unwinding: Reversing the game to allow a player to undo an unwise move. Also *Reeling Back*.

Wall: Another term for a standing stone. ▲

Of a Piece: The Origin and Meaning of
Tak Piece Shapes

Whthile much has been written about the game of Tak, relatively little has been said about the equipment used to play the game. In some ways this oversight is quite understandable, as the game is highly abstracted in its pieces. (As opposed to a game like *Fortua* where pieces are stylized to the point of archetype, and the interplay of lancers, masons, beggars, and the like create narrative as they interact.)

While the iconography of Tak is not nearly so fertile a field as *Fortua*, there are still some elements of note if we look into the provenance and cultural underpinning of some piece shapes.

Cane Pieces

The flat-bottomed round stones shown above are traditionally referred to as "cane" pieces. In recent years, some players have started to refer to them as "coins." While it is easy to assume the origin of this shape has something to do with money, quite the opposite is actually the case.

A cane or "rustic" set is made of rough circular pieces with a small slice cut off the bottom. This "foot" allows them to stand upright. Traditionally these sets were hand-made from saplings, which is doubtless where the term "cane" comes from.

True rustic sets, made from saplings, are distinguishable by their irregular sizes and curves, and have concentric rings at the center of the piece. A passage from a little-known anonymous text titled simply *Games of the Commonwealth* describes the process by which these sets were made.

> Choose a straight staff of a hard-stock tree, throughout two fingers wide, and mostly without shoots from shoulder to palm. Let stand to dry. Dress and mark it at quarter-inches, flat cut and chop the foot. Save two shorts for carving the capitals. Sand with stone or rasp, and finish with light oil for the day pieces, dark stain and oil for the night.

Aside from staining, other techniques for coloring the dark pieces include charring, and simply leaving on the bark. Of course, the two sides can also be made from different varieties of wood.

In the modern day, when manufactured sets are so easy to come by and even the most disreputable of dockside bars will likely have one, it is rare to see a true handmade cane set except as a novelty.

Manufactured cane sets are more uniform in shape, of course, and are probably more deserving of the name "coin" sets. Though honestly, at this point the terms are becoming hopelessly intermingled, and the distinctions are of interest only to those of us who care enough to vainly fight to maintain the perfect clarity of language.

Some recent works on the subject (most notably in Geoffrey Monmut's embarrassingly ill-researched and muddily worded *Tak: A Primer and Play*) have suggested the term "cane" might be descended from the ancient game called *Kaen*.

Such an assertion is, of course, foolish to the point of embarrassment. Such a mistake is understandable coming from someone of Yllish descent, who is somewhat new to the concept of the written word.

But still, a scholar whose true areas of expertise center more on fermentation, distillation, and gastronomic biology should know enough to leave this sort of work to those of us who have made genuine study of linguistics, history, and the other literary disciplines.

Tavern Pieces

These days, most easily-attainable Tak sets contain simple, square pieces. These shapes are easy to produce and inexpensive to purchase or replace. I've heard these square piece sets referred to, often in a derogatory tone, as *tavern sets* or *tavern pieces*.

Surprisingly, this derision seems to be a modern invention. In my extensive research into piece types, I discovered a handwritten disposition of a farmer, which contained the following section:

> *To myne eldest sonne Welle, I leave him the land his due. And the stock as his due. Also the hause and the appointments of the hause. It is his due, though I giff it more gladly to his family and kinde wif and wee boys than I do to him.*
>
> *But Danne shall have my prize bullock, or the sale of it, or damme all yourn eyes. And also he shall haff myne boughten tak board and bits. For while Wellie is eldest and has a wif. He has my whole life giffen me only his duty. But Danne has been the joye of myne heart. And he has broughten me gladness in these last years. I would have him take myne fyne boughten bits and remember me as he play. For Wellie, the cane is good enough for him.*

This passage suggests that at the time of this disposition, a mere 60 years ago, the cane set was seen as being less desirable than the tavern set.

Which, given your average farmer's lack of ready coin for "boughten" goods, makes a certain amount of sense.

Merchant Pieces

The familiar Cealdish trapezoid has recently become a favorite shape for Tak pieces. Anecdotally, the tradition of jot-shaped pieces originated with wealthy nobles playing Tak with money. While Cealdish coins, especially those versions from several hundred years ago, work well as pieces, it is doubtful this was ever done, especially given the disparity in the values of different metals.

It is more likely that trapezoids are preferred because of their simple, sturdy shape. They are more visually appealing than a square, and they stand more easily due to a lower center of gravity.

Their simplicity also makes them easier to produce and they are therefore cheaper than manufactured cane pieces, which require a lathe.

These factors are the more likely reason for the popularity of the Merchant shape than the idea of noble merchants playing Tak with gold.

Whatever its origin, the fact remains that the trapezoid has become the most common piece shape in Temerant.

Sometimes, full Tak sets are composed of half cane and half merchant (different shapes for different colors) to provide additional visual distinction.

All-trapezoid sets are also common, sometimes made of metals such as iron or copper. Such pieces are almost always heavily decorated or engraved, no doubt due to the terrifying anti-counterfeiting strictures set forth in the *Quiat Auriam*.

Other Pieces

Across the world, there seems to be no end to the variety of Tak piece shapes. Within the basic requirements of the game (standing, stacking, and moving without slipping apart), there is room for a good deal of artistry and craftsmanship.

In my travels I have seen Tak sets made from horn, bone, fine hardwood, and carved stone.

One particularly fine scrimshaw set was similar to a cane set, with a flat base and round top, but it had straight sides, basically a square with the top corners rounded off. The owner was a student who hailed from a coastal city to the south of Atur. He claimed it was the preferred shape where he came from, and called it a "Coluba" set.

I have seen pieces in the shape of pentagons, hexagons and octagons. Though these are usually wooden, I have seen two handsome stone sets with geometric designs, which were accompanied by cunningly worked leather boards instead of the more familiar wooden ones.

The owners of both these boards claimed that they were Yllish in origin, and while I have no evidence to substantiate this, neither do I have any reason to doubt it.

I have also known many enterprising players to commission their own sets with uniquely shaped pieces, no doubt thinking themselves the new Jezzered.

Occasionally this leads to something aesthetically pleasing. But frequently, if the designer has more creativity than sense, the pieces do not play well. The novelty of a triangular set wears off at the exact moment one's carefully constructed Lady spills unexpectedly across the board, ruining the game and costing the player a well-earned victory.

Capstones: Common and Personal

In the era of Trio and Taket, players traditionally carried their own half-sets of pieces. Today, this tradition endures in the form of unique capstones. Serious Tak players often create, trade, and even wager custom capstones in all shapes and kinds.

In a pinch, literally any small object can perform the work of a capstone. It merely needs to be a distinct shape, and capable of sitting on a stack of flat stones. So one can use almost anything: a ring, a gemstone, a die, or a figurine.

Most manufactured sets come with capstones of some appropriate size and shape, and these are suitable for some players. But many prefer to replace these caps with new pieces of a more personal nature.

Many capstones have sentimental value. Travelers sometimes keep souvenirs specifically for use as capstones, and some enterprising merchants are known to sell trinkets intended for such use.

Wealthier players, or those who play the courtly game, will sometimes collect a single theme or style of capstones, or those featuring a favorite animal, exhibiting a new one on every occasion as a dandy might exhibit a new silken doublet.

It is said that Jezzered played with an emerald capstone carved in the shape of flower, until he lost it to Breon Mercer, to whom he later referred as "a beast in the skin of a man."

I have known some players who would never deign to play for money, but who will readily play a game for a capstone.

Most frequently, this seems to be a form of social one-upmanship. I have been to several homes where players have displays of the capstones from their defeated foes.

But I have also seen this tradition turn unpleasantly mercenary when a player who could not bear to be parted from a beloved capstone was forced to ransom it back for a considerable amount of hard currency. ▲

Of a Piece: The Origin and Meaning of Tak Piece Shapes

Two Faces of Beauty:
Courtly vs. Street Tak

Tak is a singular game. Deceptively simple. Surprisingly deep. When I first read Maris Cintor's work on the subject, the game found its way into my heart and has never left.

But there is a cultural divide in the game that I rarely see discussed. Two different types of play, which I think of as courtly Tak, and street Tak.

Courtly Tak is typically played for intellectual and social gains. Games are slower. Tactics and strategy are valued. Gentility and courtesy are essential.

Street Tak is played primarily for physical or monetary gains. Games tend to be faster. Surprise and cunning are valued. Manners are more brash, and it is not uncommon for players to be bullied or insulted.

Let me stress that these different types of play have little to do with the setting. I have seen brutal, angry games played in opulent sitting rooms. I have also seen civility and grace play out across an ale-soaked tavern table.

It may seem that I am displaying a bias here, and this is true: I prefer courtly Tak. It suits my natural gifts and temperament. I enjoy considered play, gentility, and the admiration of my peers. That said, I know good players whose focus is otherwise. They love the thrill of money changing hands and

ever-doubling stakes. They play against the clock. They grant no quarter, and neither do they beg it.

Let me say this in a different way: The purpose of street Tak is *winning*. The purpose of courtly Tak is showing that you are the *better player*.

With that paradox in mind, let us examine some particular differences in these styles of play.

Street Tak

You can find a game of street Tak in any pub or tavern. It's usually the 5x5 game, but "street Tak" is more about an attitude than a set of game rules. At the very least you'll play for points, but more typically you're playing for money. Your goal is to win, as big as possible.

Players rarely call "Tak" in this environment. After all, what fool warns her opponent that she is about to win? The perfect victory is a quick, stealthy win, snapping like the jaws of a trap. If they can't see it coming, the fault lies with your victims. Sweep up your winnings and reset the board.

By the same token, turns are rarely forgiven or taken back freely, although some house rules allow a player to pay a penalty or invoke a doubling token to walk the game back.

I have known some street Tak games to be timed, though this can be cumbersome without access to a gear watch or a harmony clock. In a timed game, the emphasis is on quick wit and cunning, rather than elaborate strategy and tactics.

There is a complex game *beyond the board* in street Tak, a manipulation of advantages. Bluffs and feigned weakness. Intimidation and the use of distracting or misleading chatter.

The cost of a bottle of fine Yllish wine might be considered an investment against future winnings as you attempt to blur your opponent's wits with drink.

Because of these things, a player who loses three small wagers but scores a huge purse on the fourth game has beaten her opponent in the game beyond the board.

This is the heart of street Tak, and assuming that all parties know the rules, it can be a beautiful thing.

Courtly Tak

The civility of courtly Tak is usually reserved for the stately homes of those in high office, removed from the filth and bustle of city life.

However, as I mentioned above, some people can transcend their environment and play with class in any locale.

When playing courtly Tak, it's important to remember that the point is not strictly to win. The point is to prove that you are the better player.

This means, among other things, that you always call Tak. Warning your opponents of their predicament allows them to play their best game.

What pride is there in winning by surprise? I want my opponent to see my victory rolling toward them, brilliant and unstoppable.

Similarly, if my opponents realize they have made a mistake, they should be allowed to take back their moves, even running the game back to the beginning if appropriate.

I once saw Maris play against a skilled Modegan Lord by the name of Sovoy. They were halfway through a marvelously elaborate game when Sovoy remarked, "I'm so sorry. I made a mess with my capstone three turns back."

"I was wondering about that," Maris said. "It seemed a bad play, but I didn't know if you might have some secret hiding in the middle of it."

"No," he said. "Simple foolishness. Would you mind terribly if we reel it back a bit?"

"Not at all," she said graciously. "It seems a shame to let a blunder like that spoil so delightful a game."

They reversed their moves, then played again from the spot where Sovoy had made his error. And, in the end, Sovoy won the game.

A street player would doubtless shake his head at this. Maris could have won easily, but she didn't. Therefore, in the street player's eyes, this type of play was foolish bordering on insanity.

But courtly players vie for a different kind of win. Without Maris' permission, Sovoy couldn't have undone his mistake, and would surely have lost the game. So who was *really* in control? The person who won, or the person who allowed him to win?

I will tell you, there was no doubt among the spectators as to who had made the better showing.

Maris. Always Maris.

Think of when you last taught a new player. Was there any shame at losing to your pupil? Certainly not, because it's understood that the teacher is not playing to win. You should be proud when your student sees an opening and capitalizes on it.

This shows you are experienced enough to teach the game, wise enough to leave an opening, and humble enough to let your student win.

Though betting is not commonly a part of courtly Tak, there is still a great deal to the game *beyond the board*.

Coins do not change hands, but there is still a great deal of social currency to be won or lost.

For example, in a courtly game, the first person to play a capstone has lost a small battle.

This player is admitting that he *needs* his capstone to win, or at the very least that he is afraid of his opponent or the current situation.

In any case, when your opponent brings out his capstone first, you've scored a small victory.

You also score social points when you execute a difficult strategy against your opponent. When you trap their capstone into uselessness, or cover and capture their pieces to the point of frustration. When you push them from threat to threat, giving them no chance to recover or regroup, or transition from a Temskin defense into a Brooker's fall and thence to victory.

None of these things will put a penny in your purse, but all of them are beautiful, and each of them shows your mastery of the game to anyone who understands what they are watching.

And even if no one is watching, your opponent knows. And no matter how they might smile, you know that they know.

That is the joy of courtly Tak.

Two Faces of Beauty: Courtly vs. Street Tak

31

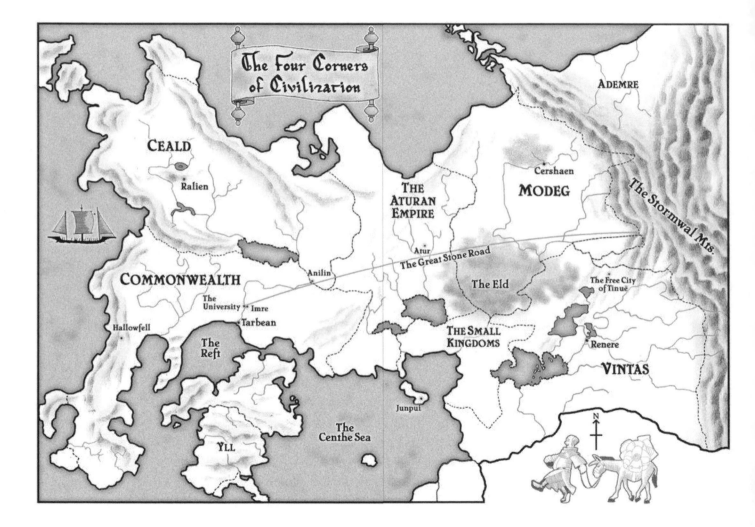

The Four Corners
of Civilization

ADEMRE

CEALD

Ralien

Cershaen

MODEG

THE
ATURAN
EMPIRE

The Stormwal Mts.

Atur

The Great Stone Road

COMMONWEALTH

Anilin

The Eld

The Free City
of Tinuë

The
University   Imre

Tarbean

Hallowfell

The
Reft

THE SMALL
KINGDOMS

Renere

VINTAS

Junpui

The
Centhe Sea

YLL

N

Customs and Variations:
Tak Around the World

T ak is known in all the four corners of the world, from The Ceald to Vintas, from Modeg to Ademre. With such a broad range, there are sure to be variations in the game from one place to the next. Below are a few examples of how the game looks and plays in different locations and cultures around the world.

Tarbean: The Fractured City

In Tarbean, the game of Tak is more or less the familiar 5x5 game, 21+1 pieces per side, using the common rules of play. However, there are several Tarbean variations on how the game is *scored*.

Throughout the city, the common gambling penalty is "Ten for the Board," meaning that the winner collects only 10 coins for the board (rather than 25), plus the count of his unplayed pieces.

While this sounds like it would make the game cheaper, it merely shifts more of the value to the pieces, rather than the board, since players choose proportionally higher stakes.

Additional penalty rules vary from place to place, and usually involve multiplying the piece value based on different special victories. The most common alternative rules are found in *Downings*, *the Tarway*, and *Middletown*.

Downings: "Double the Line." If the winning road is a *straight line*, the loser pays double the winner's piece count. For example, if a player wins with a straight line and has 7 pieces remaining, her opponent pays the usual 10 coins for the board (as mentioned above), plus 14 for the remaining pieces (7 coins doubled).

The Tarway: "Low Road, High Road." Relatively few taverns are found in the Tarway, yet it is the most densely populated region of Tak players in Tarbean. They tend to play Low Road, High Road ("Tarway Rules").

Under these rules, a player collects double for his pieces if he wins with a road entirely of height one (a *low road*), or triple if his road is entirely stacks of height two or more (a *high road*). A capstone by itself counts as a height-one stack.

If a road could take multiple paths, the winner may choose the one most favorable to him.

It is said that Breon Mercer once won a Tarway game by making both a high and low road on the same move. After some heated debate, his opponent agreed to pay him six times his piece count. However, the story also says that after that, no one in the entirety of the Tarway would play against Mercer, forcing him to leave and earn his livelihood elsewhere.

Middletown: "Double the Cap." It's assumed that Middletown rules are so called because they originated there, but this variant is actually known throughout the entirety of Tarbean, through much of the Commonwealth and Atur, and well into the Ceald.

Under these rules, a player's piece score is doubled if he wins *without playing his capstone*. So, for example, if a player wins with 4 pieces left, including his cap, the penalty for the piece count is 8 coins.

Big Middle: Players in Middletown also play the "Big Middle" rule, where winning without your Capstone entitles you to double points for the board as well as your pieces.

This is less expensive than it sounds, since Tarbean players only pay 10 points for the board. Should someone playfully suggest playing "Big Middle" with a 25-point board, especially after buying you several drinks, you should mind your purse.

These regional variations are rarely combined into one game, though they could be. Each group of players tends to treat their own home-turf rules as sacred and singular. Traditionally, if there is a conflict between multiple variants, the location of the game dictates the rules for the match.

A traveler from Middletown visiting the house of a man from Downings would play by the Downings rules. Of course, this is of little help to those of us who play outside of Tarbean, so I always advise players to agree on any variant rules before the first stone is played.

Atur: A Random Start

It is well documented that Tak players in Atur had an amusing tradition of placing their first pieces seemingly at random.

Not at all carefully either, as there are several accounts in which a player's piece finds itself off the board, on the floor, and most famously in the cleavage of a high ranking Modegan Cimbreline.

Given these hints, we believe that players were actually *pitching* their first piece onto the board, giving the game a truly random start.

There is also some indication that the position in which the pieces landed was used to determine who took the first move. Either by how well-centered in its own square the piece landed, or as Maris theorizes, by whoever's piece landed closest to the center of the board. It's also fairly clear that if a player's piece landed upright (standing) that was preferred over flat.

Today, some players at the University have taken to playing with this so-called "Aturan Start." This behavior is typically exhibited by a lower class of player preferring taverns and pubs, rather than the slightly more respectable gaming halls and cafés.

Oddly, the current fashion seems to be to throw one's *opponent's* piece in an "Aturan" start. Generally speaking, I consider what drunkards do in their own time to be their own business, but as a historian I feel the need to stress that in the classic Aturan Start, a player absolutely pitched her own piece.

Tak at the University

As mentioned above, Tak has recently undergone a renaissance among players at the University. Over the last decade, we have seen a great upwelling of interest in Tak in our corner of civilization.

Scrivs and scholars have unearthed old variants of play and attempted to decipher lost rule sets from anecdotal evidence in records.

Students specializing in advanced maths are inventing new ways to play, while rhetoricians are developing new gambits and questioning conventional modes of play.

Dozens of enthusiasts have devoted themselves to the game in recent years (your humble servant included), and nearly a hundred monographs and papers have been written on the subject (again, I must declare myself guilty). But the hub around which this activity revolves is the inestimable Maris Cintor, Re'lar.

Maris became enamored of Tak a decade ago, while attempting to reconstruct the rules to *Trio* from the scant textual evidence. In addition to her groundbreaking scholarly research on that subject, Maris has grown to be the University's preeminent Tak strategist, and is singlehandedly responsible for a complete solution to the 3x3 game.

Maris' most recent endeavor has been an attempt to calculate the ideal number of standing stones and flat stones, based on her theoretical rules for Taket, for she believes that in its era there were two distinct kinds of piece.

The core question: in an environment where a player must choose (before the game) how many of his own pieces are flat, and how many are standing, what is the right number of each?

The argument may be somewhat academic, since the rules of Taket aren't known (and likely differed from place to place). But for this research, Maris is evaluating this question in terms of the most common modern rules. And as she has a mind like no other, I eagerly await the results of her work in this area, and have no greater hope than that she call on me whensoever she could use my paltry assistance.

University Gambling Rules: "Femr's Folly"

While many at the University admire Tak as a thing unto itself, there are those among us who cannot thrill at a purely abstract pursuit. Indeed, these players routinely exhibit the compulsion to associate their prowess with some sort of material gain.

One might expect this sort of behavior to be confined to those from merchant families, tradesmen, and those of Yllish descent. But the regrettable truth is that even the sons and daughters of highly regarded families take delight in finding new ways to gamble on this noblest of games.

While several methods have been devised for wagering on Tak, one system in particular has risen to primacy since its introduction in Gerad Femr's embarrassingly titled: *"Arithmetical Assessments of Tak: Strategy, Solutions, and Schema."*

I include the rules here in an effort to be as thorough as possible, and to perform my duty as a scholar, for the benefit of future generations, setting aside my personal distaste for their author.

While it's undeniable that Femr's formulae are unassailable, even clever, I hope that I may be of value by describing his wagering schema in clear and precise terms.

Aturan, after all, is not his native language, and it has been said by many that his own explanations are, at some points, far too cunning to be understood.

Starting Wager: To begin, each player makes a wager equal to the size of the board. Typically this is a 5x5 board, so the bet is 25 coins.

Definition: A "row" of coins is equal to the width of the board. So in a 5x5 game, a "row" is 5 coins.

Starting Player: The first player is always chosen at random (not by taking turns). To counteract the first player's advantage, which Femr postulates as a 10% edge, the second player is allowed to *deduct* one row of coins from his bet.

First Tak Award: The first player to call "Tak" takes a row from the pot. (Note: Calling "Tak" is never required, except to collect this award.)

Standing Stone Penalty: The first player to play a standing stone must pay one row to the pot.

Capstone Penalty: The first player to play his capstone must pay two rows to the pot.

Reverse Moves: A player may take back one move, but must pay one row to the pot. Once a player takes back a move, the privilege to do so passes to the other player. This is tracked with a marker similar to the doubling marker in Kaen.

Endgame Award: The winner takes the pot, as well as a penalty from the loser equal to the number of pieces left in the winner's reserve. (This is the usual "board and pieces" rule.)

Flat Win Penalty: If a player wins on the flats, he must refund one row to his opponent.

Ademre: The Quiet Game

As previously described, some of Tak's earliest origins come from Ademre in the strategy game Locke. As a result, while most Adem are aware of Tak, many see the added complexity as unnecessary, and consider it a "barbarian's game."

However, I have made the effort to play Tak with several traveling mercenaries, and have spoken with others who have done the same. Their experiences mirror mine, in that we found the Adem quite skilled at the game, though they did express some unique preferences in their method of play.

The 5x5 game is the most popular, doubtless due to the similar board in Locke. However, the Adem prefer to play Tak without a capstone. On a 5x5 board, they use 22 or 24 flats, and no capstone.

I will mention a few other peculiarities of Ademic play which I find interesting, though they are not technically variants of the rules.

First, those Adem with whom I have spoken rarely wish to gamble, and when they do, it is for trivial stakes. This is true even when playing by their preferred rules, and despite the fact that they seem to be quite excellent players.

Second, it should not surprise you that the Adem do not chatter while they play. Personally, I find this refreshing, but it may disconcert players who are less familiar with their cultural foibles.

Third, the Adem take an odd pride in laying down their stones silently. Rather than calling "Tak" verbally, they place the threatening piece so as to make a quiet but audible click on the board.

Because of their play style, the Adem will find it irritating if you attempt to talk to them during the game, and especially if you click your stones down with every play. Also, if you aren't listening for their particular way of declaring a threat, it is easy to miss it, and believe that your opponent is not calling Tak at all.

I mention these details only because I believe in being as considerate as possible when playing with those from other lands who are possessed of strange customs. This is doubly true when they are well-armed and prone to violence. And I would not have you offend or irritate such dangerous persons accidentally.

Tak and the Edema Ruh

The Edema Ruh are itinerant performers. They travel the length and breadth of Temerant, moving in isolated and tight-knit family groups.

While possessed of a certain rough cunning, the Ruh are not a complex people, and are therefore ill-suited to the complicated strategies of Tak.

Notwithstanding this, many Ruh do play Tak. But the discerning player will avoid such games, especially when money is at stake. It is well known that what the Ruh cannot earn by honest labor, they will happily glean through deception, cheating, and outright theft.

Being of simple means, and not suited by their temperament to careful labor of hands, most Ruh players possess foraged or rough-made Tak sets of the "peasant" or "cane" variety, or crude things cut from bone or antler.

Should you see a Ruh with a finer set than this, it would be generous (though probably erroneous) to assume that he purchased it from a skilled craftsman, or was given it as a gift by his patron.

The Traveling Cap

The rule for the traveling (or trouper's) cap seems to have originated in Atur. But today, it's primarily attributed to the Edema Ruh, which seems to be more a romantic notion than a sensible one.

While this ancient rule has passed mostly out of fashion, it is still popular among the Ruh, and this is no doubt where they get the impression that they invented it. When playing Tak with the Ruh, it is appropriate to ask, "trouper rules?" to clarify whether the game is being played with the rules for the traveling cap.

The traveling capstone has an extra type of move: it can relocate anywhere along a road of its own color. To do this, the capstone must start and finish on a piece of its own color.

Under those conditions, the traveling cap can move, by itself, to any position on a connected string of flats, taking no pieces with it.

This odd variant rule is today seen as a novelty at best. At worst, it is a subversion of the elegance of the game. And the first time your enemy's Capstone jumps miraculously across the board, you should at least be forewarned of the possibility.

In most of Atur, asking "trouper rules?" is a small courtesy intended to prevent misunderstandings. But outside Atur, and among players of civility, it's best to remain silent on the issue. Asking the question cannot help but mark a player as embarrassingly rustic.

Concerning Tak Hustlers

While on the subject of the Edema Ruh, I feel compelled to address the broader issue of Tak hustlers, or "cleaners."

If you know anything of Tak, you know the stories of Breon Mercer, a charming rogue who traveled the world in high style, financed mainly by his winnings at Tak. Or of the legendary Teni Meran, whose unique string of victories relied little on having any skill at the game, but solely on the gullibility of the other players.

Toward the end of his life, Breon Mercer reputedly lamented that the thrill had gone out of the game, as people would line up just for the privilege of losing to him.

However, it is important to realize that while Mercer and Meran are romantic figures, there are many far more unsavory characters who follow in their footsteps in this modern day.

If you are new to the game, be wary of such people. They will frequently lose a few games at first, playing desperately and foolishly, and giving you the confidence to raise the stakes. Then the tide will turn and you will be ruined, often before you even understand what has transpired.

Their first victory will come seemingly by luck. Then they will triumph again, through some surprising gambit. And before you know it, you will be a desperate soul, doubling the stakes and begging for one more chance to get even, retiring in disgrace, and writing home to your unforgiving father, to explain why you cannot cover your term's tuition despite the ample funds he sent.

Indeed, it is not only novices who need beware.

It is comforting to imagine that all cleaners are easily spotted. As traveling scoundrels, they drift into town as loudly and obviously as the Edema Ruh. But this is sadly not the case.

Experienced players will not fall prey to grubby drifters with dust in their hair. But we can trust too much. We can be deceived with a charming Yllish accent and the promise of friendship.

So I am telling you, beware. You may think someone a colleague in scholarship. You may believe you are united in your love of the Beautiful Game. But though you might feel someone a friend, they can bide their time, gain your trust, then take unfair advantage of you when you are uncharacteristically in your cups. And while the loss of coin can be painful, it is a small defeat compared to the loss of one's dignity and innocence.

Or so I have heard. ▲

Tak in Song:
The Ballad of Teni Meran

by Molly Lewis

This song describes the strange exploits of a legendary Tak hustler. It was created for this book by songstress Molly Lewis.

Now let this poet bend your ear
Her story you should know
Of what she saw, not far from here,
And not so long ago
(And not so long ago)

In Abbot's Ford we lay our scene
A public house of brew
The stranger stood as close to me
As I am now to you.

This vagabond was gray and old
And wrinkled to his bones
But wagered he a pouch of gold
To play the game of stones

Tak, tak, the stones went down
Tak and the stones went down

The stranger threw this challenge down
His mastery to prove:
"I'll play with anyone in town
And win without a move.
Yes, I'll win without a move!"

To best a foe in such a way,
Can simply not be done
But by some ruse or clever play,
He conquered every one!

Tak, tak, the stones went down
Tak and the stones went down

Before the start of every game
He drew his rival near
Respectfully to ask his name
And whisper in his ear.

The challenger would pause in thought,
Or sometimes give a groan,
And then the stranger won the pot
And never moved a stone.

Tak, tak, the stones went down
Tak and the stones went down

As rumors of this challenge spread,
The town was thunderstruck.
"A winning streak so long," they said,
"Cannot be merely luck,
"No one could have such luck!"

He played like none had seen before
His secret no one knew.
And with each battle in the war
The sums of money grew.

Tak, tak, the stones went down
Tak and the stones went down

Does he invoke a dreadful curse
To rob his foes of breath?
Perhaps he threatens something worse
Catastrophe or death?

There's not a boy or girl alive
Who does not know these rules
Yet each opponent takes a dive
Is this a town of fools?
He must take us for fools!

At last the local champion
Agreed to join the game
"I'll hear the reason for his run,
Then thrash him all the same!"
(Hooray!) I'll thrash him all the same!

Tak, tak, the stones went down
Tak and the stones went down

"My friends," he said, "If you'll permit,
I'll make this mountebank admit
His tournament was counterfeit
His victories unreal!"

The old man swept the table clear
And beckoned his opponent near
And spoke a secret in his ear
Which I shall now reveal:

"If you should lose this game to me
And pay me for my victory,
The next game's winnings pass to thee
Now, do we have a deal?"

Our hero seemed to acquiesce
His starting moves did not impress.
But after ten stones, more or less,
The tide began to turn.

The young man did not take a fall
He laid a road and built a wall
The gathered crowd were rapt withal
To see the stranger burn.

The old man saw his act was blown
But never moved a single stone
The Hero made his victory known
His prize was fairly earned!
A fortune fairly-earned!

Tak, tak, the stones went down
Run that trickster out of town!

The people cheered to watch him go
His shoulders stooped in shame
But little did these people know
He had not lost his game.

This double-dealer's losing play
Was in his partner's plan:
She made a hundred bets that day
Against the whisp'ring man.

The sack of gold he left behind
Held pieces twenty-four,
But Teni's wagers paid in kind
And seven hundred more!

You see, my friends, you'll never cheat
A con-man at his game!
He'll make you feel you have him beat
And rob you all the same.

I stand before you humbled by
Respect for my old man.
Who handed down his methods
To the author of this plan:
Your humble balladeer, who is
The trickster Teni Meran!

Tak, tak, the stones went down
Tak and the stones went down!
Tak, tak, and the stones went down!

Brain Teasers:
Tak Puzzles

by Ira Fay

Following is a set of Tak puzzles created for this book by designer Ira Fay. In each puzzle, Black can win in one or two turns.

For simplicity, these puzzles use a 4x4 board and no capstones. They're a fun way to practice your strategy and learn the rules!

Answers are given at the end of this section.

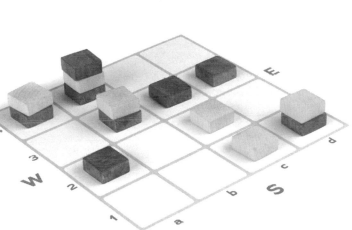

Puzzle 1: Black wins in 1

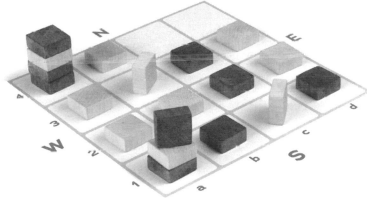

Puzzle 2: Black wins in 1

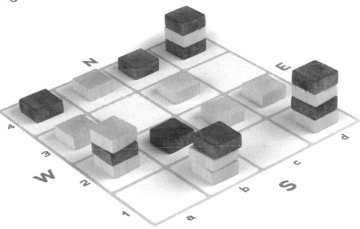

Puzzle 3: Black wins in 1

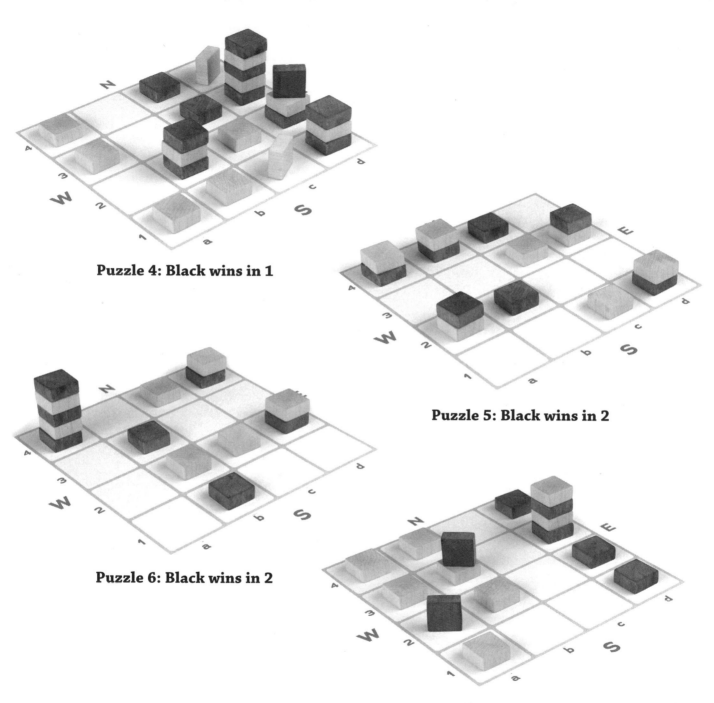

Puzzle 4: Black wins in 1

Puzzle 5: Black wins in 2

Puzzle 6: Black wins in 2

Puzzle 7: Black wins in 2

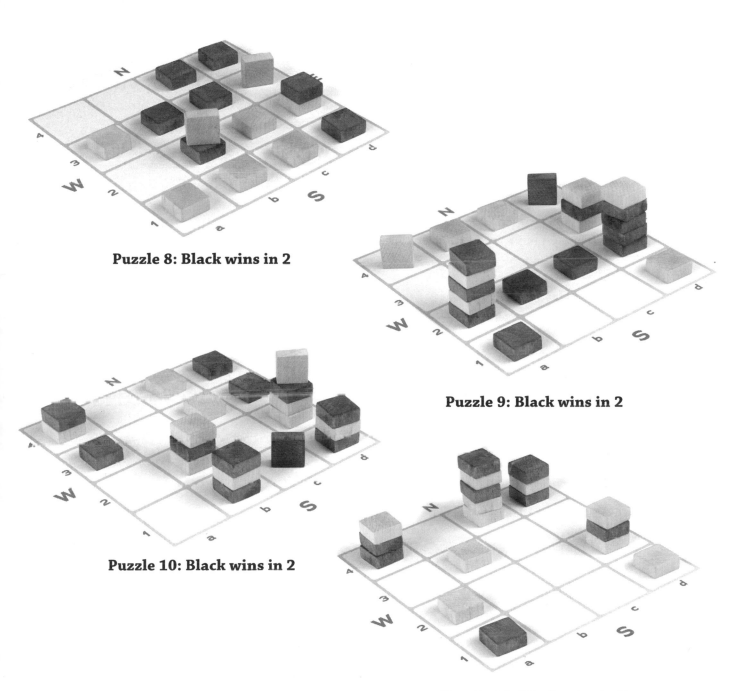

Puzzle 8: Black wins in 2

Puzzle 9: Black wins in 2

Puzzle 10: Black wins in 2

Puzzle 11: Black wins in 2

Tak Notation

Before we give the answers to the puzzles above, you'll want to learn Tak notation. This system of recording Tak games is still fairly new, having been engineered in 2016 by Tak aficionado Benjamin Wochinski (user *BenWo* on Reddit).

As in chess, each board space is designated by a letter and a number, as shown below.

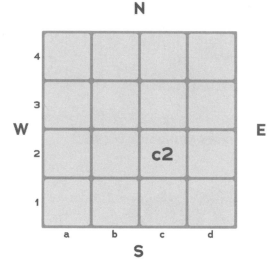

With North at the top, the cardinal directions N, S, W, and E are written either as +, -, <, and > (in text) or with arrows: ↑, ↓, ←, and →.

The simplest notation is used for the most common action: placement of a flat stone. This is just the name of the space. For example, placing a flat at c2 above would be written as "c2."

If the piece is a standing stone, add an S, as in Sc1. If the piece is a capstone, add a capital C, as in Cb2.

Movement is also written in the simplest terms possible. When moving a single piece, the only required designations are the original space and the direction. For example, moving a piece from a1 to a2 is written as "a1+" or "a1↑."

When moving a stack, beginning with a numeral indicates that you are picking up that number of pieces from the stack. (If this is obvious, the number can be ignored, such as when the stack contains only one piece).

For example, taking 3 pieces off the stack on c2 and moving them south would be written as "3c2-" or "3c2↓."

When dropping pieces as you move, the number of pieces dropped in each space along the path is written at the end of the line. Again, if this is obvious, the numbers can be omitted.

Taking four pieces from a4 and moving them east, dropping 1, 1, and 2, would be written thus: "4a4>112" or "4a4→112." The "112" at the end of this line indicates that pieces were dropped 1, 1, and 2.

What types of pieces are moving, what pieces get covered, and what other results happen (such as a capstone flattening a wall) are not included as part of this notation, because they can be derived by following the game from the beginning.

Puzzle Answers

Here are the solutions to the puzzles on pages 43-45. Of course, we suggest trying your hand at these puzzles before reading through the solutions.

Puzzle 1: 3b4↓12. Move the three stones from b4 south along the B file, leaving one stone on b3 and two stones on b2 to complete a black road from E to W.

Puzzle 2: 3a4→111. Move three stones from a4 east across the 4th rank, leaving one stone per space. This fills the board, and Black wins on flats, 7 to 6.

Puzzle 3: 3b1↑111. Move three stones on b1 north up the B file, leaving a white stone on b2, a white stone on b3, and a black stone on b4 to complete the road across the 4th rank. This also creates a road for White, but Black is the active player, so Black wins.

Puzzle 4: 2d2←. Move the top 2 stones from d2 to the west one space, uncovering the black stone on d2 to complete a black road from N to S.

Puzzle 5: c4↓. Move the stone on c4 south one space, capturing the white stone on c3. Black now threatens a road on either b3 or c2, and White can't stop both threats with a single place or move. If White blocks with 2b4↓11, Black can complete a road on a3.

Puzzle 6: 4a4↓22. Move four stones from the a4 stack south, leaving two stones on a3 and two stones on a2. That stops White's road threat on a2, and also makes a double road threat for Black on a1 or b2. White can't stop both threats.

Puzzle 7: 2b3→11. Move the stack on b3 east, leaving a white stone on c3 and capturing the stack on d3 with the black wall. White can do nothing to stop Black's next move, 2d3←, which uncovers a road on the D file. Note that White can't place a blocking wall on c3 because of the white flat stone that was left on c3 by Black's first move.

Puzzle 8: a4. Place a flat stone on a4, creating two road threats on a3 and b4. White's only way to stop both threats is to move White's wall on d3 with d3↑, but that allows Black to win with a different road by playing d3.

Puzzle 9: d4↓. Move Black's wall on d4 south one space to capture the stack on d3, which also stops White's immediate road threat. Black now threatens a road by 3d3↓12, which would leave a black stone on d2 to complete the road on the 2nd rank. White could move the large stack on d2, but a black stone would inevitably be left behind on d2, due to the carry limit of 4 stones. If the white stone ends on b2 or c2, Black recaptures and completes the road with 4a2→22. If the white stone ends on a2, Black recaptures with a1↑.

Puzzle 10: 2b1↑. Move two stones from the b1 stack north one space, threatening a road on either a2 or b3. White's only way to stop both threats is to move white's wall on d2 to capture the b2 stack, but that allows black to win with a road on the D file with 2d1↑.

Puzzle 11: 4c4←22. Move four stones from the c4 stack west, leaving two stones on b4 and two on a4. This move leaves a white stone on c4 due to the carry limit, but it creates two road threats for Black: one along the 4th rank with 2d4← (or 4a4→13) and the other along the A file with 4a4↓13. White cannot stop both roads in a single move.

Game Rules II:
Rules for Kaen and Locke

by James Ernest

Kaen and Locke are real games, created for this booklet. Below are the rules to both, as well as a short article about Patrick Rothfuss' early concepts for Tak.

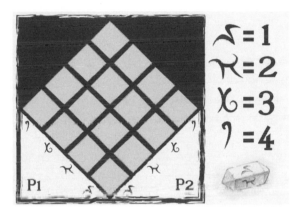

$\mathcal{S}$ = 1
$\mathcal{R}$ = 2
$\mathcal{Y}$ = 3
$\mathcal{l}$ = 4

How to Play Kaen

Kaen, also known as "From the Earth to the Sky," is the oldest known road-building game in Temerant, and is seen as a precursor to modern Tak.

The board is a diamond-shaped 4x4 grid, shown above, with the bottom edges representing "Earth" and the top edges representing "Sky."

The goal is to build a *bridge* connecting Earth to Sky. This is a line of orthogonally connected spaces that joins two opposite sides of the board, which is exactly the same as a road in Tak.

However, the *true* goal of the game is to win money, and there are several ways for the game to end without a finished bridge.

Components: You need a game board, money for betting, a die, a doubling marker, and about ten stones per player (Tak pieces work nicely).

Board: A 4x4 Tak board is adequate for this game, but it's better if you can mark it with symbols to match the die, as shown at left.

Money: Whether playing for real money or just keeping score, you'll need about 100 chips or coins for each player.

Hut (Die): A traditional hut is marked with the four symbols that designate the rows and columns of the board, as shown at left. Of course, any 4-sided die will do.

Doubling Marker: This can be any object, such as a Tak capstone. This marker represents *permission to double*, and starts in a neutral state (i.e., granting permission to both players).

When a player offers to *double*, the doubling marker passes to her opponent. Only that player can make the next offer to double, by passing it back, and so on. The marker returns to a neutral state at the end of each game.

To Begin

Players choose opposite sides of the diamond board. Clear the board and place the doubling marker in a neutral spot. On the first game, start with a random player. In subsequent games, start with the *loser* of the previous game.

Each player makes the same starting bet, for example 2 chips. This bet should be a multiple of 2, because sometimes players can retrieve half of their bet.

Keep the two players' bets in separate stacks, as each bet may change independently during the play of the game.

The total chips in play including both players' bets are collectively called the "pot."

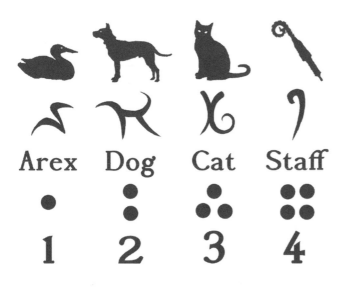

Symbol sets from ancient and modern Kaen

On Each Turn

Usually, you start your turn by rolling the die. (Other options are listed under "Before the Roll.")

Your roll gives you permission to place a stone in an empty space in the indicated row. One player's rows are the other player's columns. (See the board diagrams on the following page.) For example, if you roll a 2, you can play a stone in any empty space in your "2" row.

Full Row: If you can't place a piece, because the designated row is full, you must choose one of these two options: you may forfeit the game, or you may *match your bet* and continue.

"Matching" your bet means adding more money equal to the current size of your bet. For example, if your bet stands at 4, you must add another 4 to make it 8. You will place no stone on this turn, and the turn passes to your opponent.

Bridge Win: If you complete a bridge, you win the game and collect the pot. (A bridge is a string of pieces connecting two opposite sides of the board, exactly like a road in Tak.)

Full Board: If the board is filled, the game is over. If no one has made a bridge, then the player with more pieces in play is the winner.

If the number of pieces in play is tied, then the players divide the money in the pot. (This is not the same as each player retrieving his bet, because the bets can change size independently.)

Before the Roll

You have two options before you roll the die. You can *double* or *surrender*.

Double: If you have the doubling marker, or if it is neutral, you may offer it to your opponent. They may either accept the offer, or forfeit the game.

If they accept, *both players double their current bet*, and the game continues. You then proceed to roll the die as usual.

Obviously you will double when you think you are in a strong position to win.

Surrender: If you don't like your odds of winning, you can surrender *before you roll*. In this case, take back half your total bet, and forfeit the game.

Keeping Score

This is a gambling game, so the long-term goal is to finish with more money than you started with. If you wish to play a series of fixed length, choose a number of games and then compare your holdings at the end. You will have to decide whether a player is eliminated when she runs out of money, or if she can reload.

One option when a player is out of chips is to reload both players and double the stakes! This is more practical when you are playing only for points; when playing for money, each game should be considered independent, and the stakes should be chosen at the start of each game.

Example Game

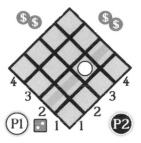

On the first turn, both players make an initial bet of $2. Player 1's first roll is a 2, so he can place a stone in any spot along his row 2. He places at (2,3), as shown here.

In Kaen you are often making strategic decisions between completing your own bridge and blocking your opponent's bridges and rows.

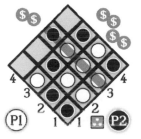

For the first few rounds, placement is normal. Then Player 2 rolls a 3, selecting a row that is already full. She could forfeit now, but she chooses to match her bet.

The strategy behind this decision is that for P2, three rows are still open. For P1, three rows are blocked. This means P1 is far more likely to get stuck with a bad roll. And at this point in the game, neither player can complete a bridge.

On the next turn, P1 rolls a 1, and is indeed blocked. He could have surrendered before the roll, taking back $1 and losing only $1. Now he has to decide whether to forfeit (losing $2) or put out another $2.

Since on the next turn P2 will probably double, P1 decides that his best odds are to forfeit rather than paying the extra $2 on this turn. This ends the game, and P2 collects the pot of $6.

How to Play Locke

Locke, also called "Centerline," is a quick-playing strategy game, played on a 5x5 board with ten pieces per player. Locke has its roots in Ademre, and is still played there, though not widely.

Equipment: A 5x5 board and ten pieces per player.

Your pieces can be anything: Tak pieces, pebbles, buttons, or coins. It's not necessary that the pieces be able to stack, but it's nice if they can.

When the pieces don't stack, the Locke board can be made with shallow wells rather than flat spaces, to keep multiple pieces grouped in the same spot. This can be accomplished by carving wells in wood or stone, or just by making divots in the ground.

Setup: Each player starts with eight pieces on the board, arranged as shown in the diagram at right. Your other two pieces start in reserve.

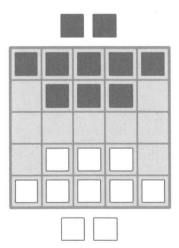

The starting setup for Locke

Starting Player: On the first game, play begins with a random player. On subsequent games, the loser of the previous game goes first.

Object: The object of the game is to occupy *any three spaces* along the middle row.

Stacking: Pieces of the same color can stack up, creating larger and more powerful stacks. The maximum size of a stack is 3 pieces.

Each Turn: On your turn, you will usually *move* one of your stacks (a "stack" can be size 1, 2, or 3). Instead of moving, you may play one piece from your reserve into an empty space in your first row.

Movement: Different-sized stacks can move and capture in different ways. In general, pieces can move into an empty space, or they may combine with allied pieces, up to a maximum stack size of 3.

Stacks can move a distance up to their size (1 space for a stack of 1, etc.), along a straight, open path. There are no jumps and no diagonal moves.

A stack can *capture* a stack that is *exactly* 1 piece smaller than it (for example, a 3 can capture a 2).

Capturing: Captured stacks are knocked out of play. When a stack is captured, its component pieces return to their owner's reserve, from which they can be put back into play one at a time.

Playing a New Piece: On your turn, rather than making a move, you may play a piece from your reserve into an empty space on your first row.

Rules for Move and Capture

One Piece: A stack of one piece can move one space, either into empty space, or to combine with an allied stack of height 1 or 2. Stacks of height 1 can't capture.

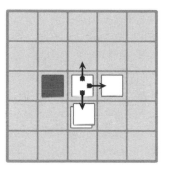

Two Pieces: A stack of two can move one or two spaces, either into empty space, or to combine with an allied stack of height 1. Stacks of height 2 can capture enemy stacks of height 1.

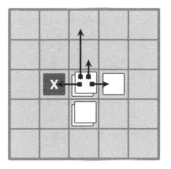

Three Pieces: A stack of three pieces moves up to three spaces. It can't combine with more pieces, because the maximum size is 3. Stacks of height 3 can only capture enemy stacks of height 2.

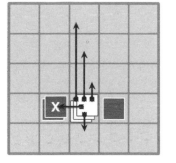

Starvation Rule: You lose the game if, at the end of a turn, you have fewer than three stacks in play.

No Reverse Moves: It is not legal to make a move that is the exact reverse of your previous move.

Stalemate: If both players repeatedly choose to loop the game back to a prior game state, this is a stalemate. In this case, the game is a draw.

Modern Variations of *Locke*

Locke is still played today, primarily in Ademre, where it is occasionally referred to as *Llean*. Elsewhere in the world, it is also called *Centerline*.

Players commonly use Tak pieces and Tak boards, so pieces can be stacked rather than grouped. This is why we describe the groups of pieces as "stacks," and not "groups."

In the modern game, there is no limit to the height of a stack, and every stack can still capture only a stack that is one piece smaller.

Modern players sometimes play with 12 or 14 pieces, with the extras starting in reserve. These pieces aid in the creation of taller stacks, so this feeds nicely into a game with no stack limit.

Bonus: Patrick's Tak Rules

Before I ever got involved, Patrick Rothfuss took a crack at designing Tak. This was back in 2007, while he was still working on *The Wise Man's Fear*.

Pat wanted to write intelligently about the game, even if he didn't explain the rules, and he knew this would be easier if he had a real game.

Through this process, Pat discovered that game design was trickier than he thought. His first three games ended in a perfect tie, including the game where he was *actively trying to lose*.

Pat sat down recently and showed me some of the concepts that he incorporated into his original Tak concept. Like the final game, the original Tak concepts were played with colored stones on a square gridded board.

Influence

The core concept of "Pat Tak" revolves around *influence*. You want to build networks of pieces that exert influence over spaces on the board. Influence dictates the areas where you and your opponent are allowed to play. The goal is area control: in short, you want to play more pieces onto the board than your opponent.

A single pieces exerts one point of influence into the four adjacent spaces (fig. 1). A line of pieces has more power in the direction of the line.

Depending on the variant, that influence was stacked up in a single spot (fig. 2) or drawn out farther along the line (fig. 3).

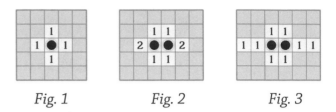

| Fig. 1 | Fig. 2 | Fig. 3 |

Influence dictates where you can place stones. You can't build where your opponent has more influence than you. (If it's tied, as with an empty space, either player can build there.)

By stacking pieces, you create stronger influence in a closer space. For example, a stack of 3 pieces exerts three points of control in the four neighboring spaces (fig. 4).

Fig. 4

The crucial aspect of influence is that, if strong enough, it can actually remove opposing pieces from the board.

These pieces are probably captured, as in chess, rather than returned to the infinite supply, as in go. But again, this game was in a formative state when it was abandoned, so many variations are possible.

Pat played very little with this game concept, and no written rules survive. One might consider it a design project waiting for a designer, or just one of the steps on the road to Tak. ▲

About the Creators:
Who is Responsible for This?

This book was created by Patrick Rothfuss and James Ernest, and illustrated by Nate Taylor. Here is a bit more about them.

James Ernest

James Ernest is a game inventor and graphic designer best known as the president of Cheapass Games. He has invented more than 150 original tabletop and digital games, ranging across many genres and formats.

He started his career in the game industry in 1993 as a technical writer for Wizards of the Coast. His jobs at Wizards included re-writing the rules for *Magic: the Gathering* four times.

In 1996, James Ernest founded Cheapass Games, a low-budget game company famous for requiring their players to provide generic spare parts like dice, pawns, and play money. Cheapass released a variety of original games at rock-bottom prices, including *Kill Doctor Lucky*, *Button Men*, *BRAWL*, *Unexploded Cow*, and *Lord of the Fries*.

In 2007, James took a job at Microsoft, as game design manager for Carbonated Games, overseeing many digital projects including *Hexic 2*, *UNO Rush*, and the *Fable II Pub Games*.

After several years in the digital world, James returned to tabletop games, rebooting Cheapass Games through Kickstarter with a deluxe reprint of *Unexploded Cow*. Ironically, the new Cheapass Games makes mostly deluxe games (some original, like *Tak*, and some reprints, like *Kill Doctor Lucky*). But they also offer many of their older titles in free print-and-play versions.

James gives frequent design lectures at colleges and conventions, and he helped design the current curriculum for DigiPen's introduction to tabletop game design. After Tak, his next project will be a textbook on tabletop game design.

James lives in Seattle with his wife Carol and their daughter Nora, and in his spare time he builds LEGO models and tries to win money at poker.

Patrick Rothfuss

Patrick Rothfuss was born in Madison, Wisconsin, to awesome parents. After nine years at the University of Wisconsin-Stevens Point, he accidentally gained enough credits to graduate with an English degree. Pat then went to grad school.

When the voices told him to, Pat left home to attend college at University Wisconsin-Stevens Point, where he joined Slytherin house and had many wonderful adventures. After graduating, Pat evolved into a being of pure light and energy.

Then he went to grad school and evolved even further into a being composed entirely of bile, rage, binder twine, and sweet, sweet, methadone. After grad school, Pat joined forces with five plucky Japanese schoolgirls to form a giant robot that fights crime.

As you probably know if you're reading this, he's published some books, too. Most notably: *The Name of the Wind*, *The Wise Man's Fear*, and *The Slow Regard of Silent Things*. His Kingkiller Chronicle series has been translated into over 35 languages, won many awards, hit many bestseller lists, and sold many millions of copies.

As you may *not* know, he's also written two not-for-children picture books called *The Adventures of the Princess and Mr. Whiffle*, illustrated by the illustrious Nate Taylor.

They're fun, but hard to find. You can get them signed over at **TheTinkersPacks.com**.

In 2008, Pat accidentally founded a charity called Worldbuilders, which rallies the geek community in an attempt to make the world a better place.

Over the years, Worldbuilders has raised over $5,000,000, vastly improving the lives of thousands of families around the world. If you're curious, you can find more info at **worldbuilders.org**.

Though he no longer teaches at the university, Pat continues to live in Stevens Point, where he cuddles his children, tells stories about life on his blog, and just generally dicks around on the internet.

Nate Taylor

Nate Taylor has been an artist his entire life, but only recently started doing it professionally.

He originally wanted to be an animator, which compelled him to study motion and cartooning. But Nate lacked the patience for actual animation, so he shifted his focus to illustration, to create art for movie posters.

He got his first art degree at Washington State University, where he met another artist and writer, Patrick Johnson. The two of them collaborated on many unpublished projects and became friends with Patrick Rothfuss, who was doing his graduate studies at WSU.

In 2006, Nate got published for the first time, and produced the map of the Four Corners for the Kingkiller Chronicle.

In 2007, Nate co-created the webcomic *Coming Distractions* with Patrick Johnson, and the two of them kept it going for four years. During the same time, Patrick Rothfuss approached Nate to illustrate *The Adventures of the Princess And Mr. Whiffle*. The book was released in 2010, and Nate began working as an artist in mobile games in 2011.

Nate left the game industry just in time to start working on the second Princess And Mr. Whiffle book, and his career was starting to gain traction. After completing *The Dark of Deep Below* in 2012, Nate met James Ernest, and he began contributing to the *Pairs* game that James was producing with Patrick. At the same time, he created the cover for John Scalzi's compilation *The Mallet of Loving Correction* for Subterranean Press.

Since then, Nate has worked with Patrick Rothfuss on the comic book *So Long As You Can See the Moon,* for the game *Torment: Tides of Numenera*, and he illustrated *The Slow Regard of Silent Things*. He and Pat Johnson also Kickstarted a book compilation of their *Coming Distractions* comic series.

Nate has worked with Shawn Speakman, contributing art for *Unfettered II* and the *Broken Empire* omnibus, and he's illustrating the new edition of Terry Brooks' *Sometimes the Magic Works*.

When not drawing, Nate enjoys movies, quantum theory, and games.

Tak: A Beautiful Game
Credits

Tak is not actually a thousand years old, and Daramin Centes is not a real person. Instead, we are grateful to many real live contributors to this book, including:

Book Text:
Patrick Rothfuss and James Ernest

Game Design:
James Ernest and Patrick Rothfuss

Playtesters:
Boyan Radakovich, Paul Peterson, Rick Fish, Jeff Morrow, Jeff Wilcox, Joseph Kisenwether, Craig Stockwell, and many many others!

Edited by:
Carol Monahan and Cathy Saxton

Front Cover and Interior Art:
Nate Taylor

Back Cover:
Pete Venters

Tak Pieces and Photos:
James Ernest

Puzzle Design:
Ira Fay; testing by Josh Brannon, Gabe Cohn, David Cornwell, Alex Fay, Marshall Fay, Tom Gale, Hawkbat, Patricia Komoda, Maron, Brandon Patton, Shawn Patton, Nick Peeples, Sam Thibault, Ben Wochinski, Eric Zeller

Tak Notation:
Ben Wochinski

The Ballad of Tak:
Molly Lewis and James Ernest

Special Thanks:

The first edition of Tak was made possible by a Kickstarter campaign, run by Cheapass Games in the spring of 2016. The campaign raised $1.35M from 12,000 backers, and this book was part of the reward structure.

Our deepest thanks to the enthusiastic and patient backers who made this possible, and to the staff at Cheapass Games and Elodin Enterprises:

Cheapass Games:
James Ernest
Carol Monahan
Cassidy Werner

Elodin Enterprises:
Patrick Rothfuss
Amanda Hoerter
Mindy McCord

Other Resources:

Patrick Rothfuss and James Ernest are both clever enough to have their own URLs:
patrickrothfuss.com
jamesernest.com

The newest information about Tak can be found at:
jamesernest.com/games/tak